baseball's new wave

Ichiro Suzuki

Best in the West

BY
MARK STEWART

THE MILLBROOK PRESS
BROOKFIELD, CONNECTICUT

M

THE MILLBROOK PRESS

Produced by
BITTERSWEET PUBLISHING
John Sammis, President
and
TEAM STEWART, INC.
RESEARCHED AND EDITED BY MIKE KENNEDY

Series Design and Electronic Page Makeup by
JAFFE ENTERPRISES
Ron Jaffe

All photos courtesy AP/ Wide World Photos, Inc., except the following:
SportsChrome — Cover
Kyodo News — Pages 6, 8, 11, 12, 13 (both), 15 top, 16, 18, 21
The following images are from the collection of Team Stewart:
Topps Chewing Gum, Inc. © 1978—Page 9 top
The Topps Company, Inc. © 2001—Page 27 bottom
The Upper Deck Company LLC © 2001—Page 29
Fleer/Skybox International LC © 2000—Page 33 top
Select Publications, Inc. © 1951—Page 37 bottom
ESPN, Inc. © 2001—Page 39
Legends Publishing Group, Inc. © 2001 —Page 40
Manufacturer Unknown © 1928—Page 41
Legends Publishing Group, Inc. © 2001—Page 45 (Suzuki)
Topps Chewing Gum, Inc. © 1964—Page 45 (Oliva)
Wilson Meats, Inc. © 1954—Page 45 (Kuenn)
Goudey Gum Company © 1937—Page 45 (Waner)
Frank H. Fleer Corporation © 1961—Page 45 (Alexander)
Manufacturer Unknown © 1928—Page 45 (Frederick)

Printed in the United States of America

Published by
The Millbrook Press, Inc.
2 Old New Milford Road
Brookfield, Connecticut   06804
www.millbrookpress.com

Library of Congress Cataloging-in-Publication Data

Stewart, Mark.
  Ichiro Suzuki : best in the west / by Mark Stewart.
    p. cm. — (Baseball's new wave)
Includes index.
Summary: A biography of the Seattle Mariners hitting and fielding star who won
the MVP and Rookie of the Year Award in 2001 and became the first successful
Japanese player in the Major Leagues.
  ISBN 0-7613-2616-2 (lib. bdg.)
  1. Suzuki, Ichiro, 1973—-Juvenile literature. 2. Baseball
players—Japan—Biography—Juvenile literature. [1. Suzuki, Ichiro, 1973- 2.
Baseball players. 3. Japan—Biography.] I. Title. II. Series.
  GV865.S895 S74 2002
  796.357'092—dc21
                                                        2002003343

1 3 5 7 9 10 8 6 4 2

Contents

Rising Son

chapter | 1

> "Baseball has been the
> greatest thing in my life."
> — ICHIRO SUZUKI

As near as anyone can tell, the first baseball to arrive on Japanese shores was among the possessions of a teacher named Albert Bates. He traveled to Tokyo by steamship in 1873, and while he was instructing university students in English, he also taught a group of them how to play the curious bat-and-ball game. The Japanese found baseball to be perfectly suited to their culture. It demanded a dedication to individual excellence, yet everything was done within a well-defined framework of team play.

In the years that followed, Japan grew from a mysterious and reclusive island nation into a world economic power. Today, there is probably not a single home in North America that does not contain something that was made there; the Japanese manufacture

American baseball arrived in Japan during the 1870s. It took more than a century for the first Japanese MVP, Ichiro Suzuki, to arrive in America.

Ichiro's father, Nobuyuki, dedicated many years to making his son a complete player.

almost every type of product imaginable. About the only thing Japan did not export to this continent was a baseball superstar.

When Ichiro Suzuki was growing up, he wondered why this was. Japan's baseball heroes looked every bit as good to him as the major leaguers he saw on television. The explanation he received was that the average Western player was bigger and stronger and faster than the average Japanese player. That may have been true, but what about the very biggest and best Japanese stars—weren't they good enough to make it in the majors?

They may well have been. But the rules in Japanese baseball were very strict. Players were bound to their teams for many, many years. This meant they could not sign with North American ball clubs until they were past their prime years. By that time, the best players were too comfortable with their fame to leave Japan for a tougher game and an alien culture. Also, many so-so major leaguers had come to Japan and become stars. This made people believe that a Japanese star would only be a so-so player in North America.

Ichiro's father, Nobuyuki Suzuki, had big dreams for his son. He wanted Ichiro to have a good career in Japanese baseball. The owner of a small cooler repair factory, Nobuyuki was used to making plans and following them closely. He made his plan for Ichiro, and within a few years he was the best young player in his home city of Toyoyama.

Ichiro got his first baseball glove when he turned three years old. He batted right-handed and had excellent hand-eye coordination. Ichiro's father assumed that his boy would be quick and strong (as *he* had been in his youth), so he made him into a left-handed hitter. A lefty with speed has a much better chance of beating out slow ground balls—and stretching singles into doubles—because he is a step or two closer to first base when he completes his swing.

Ichiro joined his first organized team in 1980, at the age of six. It was sponsored and coached by his father. The games were played on Sundays, but father and son practiced hitting, fielding, and pitching each day on a nearby elementary school field, and also made regular visits to a batting range. Ichiro would start on the slower machines, then move to progressively faster ones. When he got to the fastest

Ichiro became a left-handed hitter as a boy to take advantage of his speed. The idea was his father's

machine, he would move progressively closer in order to speed up his swing.

Nobuyuki also taught his son important lessons about fitness and good eating. There would be no American junk food in his diet—just a lot of protein and vitamins.

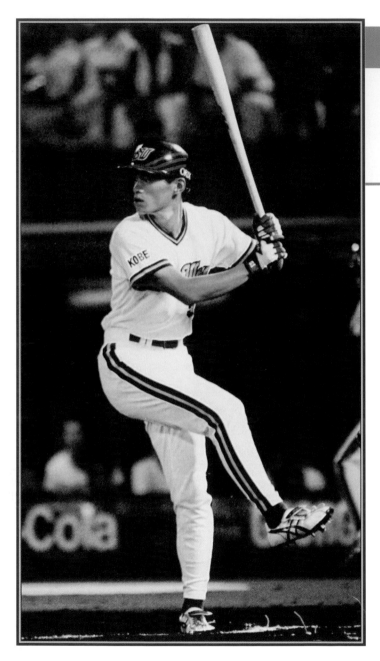

Ichiro was a wiry kid, and his father wanted him to grow up strong. His aunt made a soup with special muscle-building ingredients, and he gulped it down by the bowlful. If a meal did not meet Nobuyuki's strict standards, he would forbid his son to eat it.

During the 1980s, Ichiro became something of a child celebrity in Japanese baseball circles. Wherever he played, he hit beautifully, fielded stylishly, and ran the bases with abandon. He was also one heck of a pitcher. By his teen years, Ichiro was reaching 90 mph on the radar gun. His father saw that he maintained his rigorous training schedule, both on and off the diamond. He also made sure Ichiro had the best equipment money could buy.

The coach at Aiko-Dai Meiden High School could hardly wait for Ichiro to enroll. When he did the team became a national powerhouse. Ichiro did it all. On the mound,

FROM ACROSS THE OCEAN

Ichiro first started wondering about what it would be like to play baseball on the other side of the Pacific while he was in high school. During this time, several American players enjoyed productive years in the Japanese Leagues. Among them were ex-major leaguers Jim Paciorek, Boomer Wells, and Ralph Bryant, former All-Star Larry Parrish, and Warren Cromartie, who wrote a book about his experience in Japan.

Expos
WARREN CROMARTIE

he was more than just a "thrower"—he seemed to know what batters were expecting, and had the talent and control to deliver pitches they had little chance of hitting. At the plate, Ichiro would "set up" pitchers to throw the pitch he wanted, in the location he wanted, at the speed he wanted. Sometimes this meant fouling off many pitches. But Ichiro had such great bat control he could chip away endlessly until the enemy hurler finally gave in.

Ichiro graduated from high school in 1991 and prepared to begin his professional career. No one questioned his skills, but his size was a matter of considerable concern. He stood 5 feet 9 inches (175 centimeters), and tipped the scales at just over 150 pounds (68 kilograms). To pass him on the street, you would never have known he was a future baseball star. Because of his small stature, most teams had the teenager listed as a pitcher. On draft day, Ichiro was shocked when several rounds went by and he did not hear his name called. It seemed that no one was in the market for a skinny pitcher.

> "In our fathers' generation, baseball was huge... it was a father's dream for his boy to be a baseball player."
> **HIDE SUEYOSHI, MARINERS EXEC (behind Ichiro in photo)**

Breaks of the Game

chapter 1

"He didn't realize what he had."

— SPORTSWRITER WAYNE GRACZYK, ON ICHIRO'S FIRST MANAGER

The Orix Blue Wave of Japan's Pacific League decided to take a chance on Ichiro Suzuki, and claimed him in the fourth round. However, when he arrived in training camp, he was practically laughed off the field. The manager, Shozo Doi, and his coaches thought Ichiro looked like a little boy. After watching him throw off the mound, they decided he was too small for the position and waved him to the outfield. Later, when they saw his high leg kick at the plate, they shook their heads and sent him to the club's farm team. Before Ichiro packed his bags, Doi pulled him aside and said, "You'll never hit."

Doi probably thought he would never see Ichiro again. But as often happens, injuries on the big-league roster created a need for an extra outfielder. In 1992

Did You Know?

The Orix Blue Wave play their home games in the city of Kobe. The team has been owned by Orix (a large leasing company) since 1988. Prior to that they were owned by Hankyu Railways. In Japan, a baseball team is identified with its owner, not the city in which it plays.

Akira Ogi, the manager who first understood Ichiro's potential.

and 1993, Ichiro was called up to the Blue Wave for a total of 83 games. He barely got to play, mostly because Doi wanted to prove to the team that it had made a mistake in drafting him. "He didn't like Ichiro's stance, his looks, the way he batted," remembers Wayne Graczyk, who worked as sports editor for *The Tokyo Weekender* at the time.

When the 1993 season ended, Ichiro joined a newly formed winter league in Hawaii. The Blue Wave sent several young players from its organization to the Hilo Stars, and they led the team to the league title. Ichiro got to play every day, develop his skills, and test himself against some young American prospects. He gained much confidence playing away from Japan (and away from Doi). Ichiro finished among the leaders in RBIs and had a .311 batting average—fifth best in the league and more than 100 points higher than he had hit for the Blue Wave in 1993.

As Ichiro prepared to start the 1994 season, he got a piece of excellent news: Orix had fired Doi and replaced him with a man named Akira Ogi to manage the team. This was very unexpected. The Blue Wave had finished with a winning record in 1993, just 3.5 games out of first place.

One of the new skipper's first moves was to make twenty-year-old Ichiro his right fielder. When he watched the kid's wacky swing, he noticed that he made a lot of minute adjustments just before his bat swooshed through the hitting zone. That told him he might have a very special player on his hands.

Ichiro started pounding out hits at a record-breaking rate. In a league dominated by pitching, it was considered quite a feat to bat .300—and no one had ever rapped out

*Ichiro is congratulated by his Blue Wave teammates. He won
the MVP award in his first full season with the team.*

200 hits. Ichiro was hitting close to .400 all year, and had surpassed the 100-hit level before midseason. His consistency was incredible. He never suffered a slump, and from May 21 to August 26 (a span of 69 games!) he reached base at least once in every single contest.

Aside from Ichiro, the Blue Wave had a balanced attack. It included Hirofumi Ogawa and Junichi Fukura, who, like Ichiro, were line-drive hitters. The team's power was supplied by Ty Gainey, a former Houston Astro, and Francisco Cabrera, whose ninth-inning single had won the 1991 National League pennant for the Atlanta Braves. Both players were in Japan trying to restart their careers. The Blue Wave's best pitchers were Yoshinori Sato, Nobuyuki Hoshino, and staff ace Shigetosi Hasegawa.

Junichi Fukura, one of three Blue Wave players to top the .300 mark in 1994.

Orix had a good team, but the Seibu Lions had a better one. The 1993 champions defended their title and won the Pacific League championship easily. The Blue Wave ended up in a tie for second. As for Ichiro, he finished as the Pacific League batting leader, outdistancing runner-up Kazunori Yamamoto by the incredible margin of .385 to .317. He also set a new record with 210 hits, finished second in steals, won a Gold Glove for his fielding, and was named Most Valuable Player.

As amazing as these achievements were for a young man of twenty, they paled in comparison to the national mania that surrounded him. Japan was obsessed with Ichiro. His assault on the .400 mark gripped the country, while his boyish charm and innocence made him a heartthrob for millions of female fans. Another young player might have folded up with all this attention, but it turned out Ichiro was a natural ham. He knew just when to smile, just what to say, and had a marvelous sense of showmanship. When crowds started chanting *I-chi-ro* during his at bats, he would take his time stepping into the batter's box so he could let the noise build. Between innings, while his pitcher warmed up, Ichiro would sometimes play catch with the fans in the stands— not the right field stands, but the left-field stands!

"Ichiro-mania" gripped Japan during the 1990s.

Pacific Heights

chapter

"He's one of the top 10 offensive players in the world."

— BOBBY VALENTINE, FORMER
LOTTE MARINES MANAGER AND
CURRENT NEW YORK METS MANAGER

In the months between the 1994 and 1995 baseball seasons, the Ichiro craze continued to grow. Photos, buttons, jewelry, banners, trading cards—anything bearing the image of Japan's young superstar just flew off store shelves. The kid with the big kick and bazooka arm had turned baseball upside down, and many wondered what he could possibly do to match the amazing feats of his first full season.

Ichiro certainly knew. The Blue Wave had never finished first in the Pacific League and had never played in the Japan Series. The Japan Series is

Did You Know?

In 1995, Hideo Nomo of the Kintetsu Buffaloes was signed by the Los Angeles Dodgers. Nomo, who led the Pacific League in victories from 1990 to 1993, went 13–6, led the National League in strikeouts, and was named Rookie of the Year. Never before had a Japanese player made such an impact in the majors.

Shigetosi Hasegawa, star hurler of the Blue Wave. He would go on to play for the Anaheim Angels.

like our World Series; it pits the Pacific League and Central League pennant-winners in a best-of-seven contest. As training camp began, Ichiro looked around and saw a team that was close to taking that major step. Once again, Shigetosi Hasegawa led a solid pitching staff, which also included Nobuyuki Hoshino and Koji Noda. The team's core of line-drive hitters was back again, too. Most important, two new Americans had joined the Blue Wave. Japanese teams are limited to just a handful of foreign players, and Orix rarely got good ones. This year, they had signed a couple of former Oakland A's, Doug Jennings and Troy Neel. Both were accomplished hitters.

Ichiro especially wanted to win the pennant for the team's home city of Kobe. That January, a magnitude 7.2 earthquake struck without warning, toppling hundreds of structures and killing more than 6,000 people. The city started a campaign called the "Kobe Comeback." The Blue Wave players wore sleeve patches that read *Gambarou Kobe*, which means "Let's Do Our Best for Kobe!"

In a season that stood the Pacific League on its head, the two perennial also-rans—the Orix Blue Waves and Chiba Lotte Marines—finished atop the standings. The Marines' success was attributed to their dynamic

Kobe residents needed something to cheer for after the earthquake that devastated their city.

Ichiro heads for home in a 1995 game. His team reached the Japan Series, but lost to the Yakult Swallows.

American manager, Bobby Valentine. He got excellent seasons from All-Star Kiyoshi Hatsushiba and a couple of American stars, Julio Franco and Pete Incaviglia. The Marines, however, finished second to the surprising new league champion Blue Wave—led by Ichiro, who won the batting title and MVP again. The young star topped the Pacific League in hits, runs, RBIs, stolen bases, on-base percentage, total bases, and being hit by a pitch. Ichiro also clubbed 25 home runs. By restoring pride to a city that had literally been torn to pieces, Ichiro became a national hero.

Unfortunately, Ichiro's season ended just short of where he had hoped. The Blue Wave faced the Yakult Swallows in the Japan Series, who were just too much for them. The Swallows won the first three games in the best-of-seven series, behind the hitting

of Central League MVP Tom O'Malley and the pitching of Terry Bross. A pair of home runs by Jennings gave Orix a win in Game Four and a glimmer of hope, but Bross slammed the door on Ichiro and his teammates the next day to take the series.

When the Blue Wave regrouped for the 1996 campaign, all the key players were back. Neel and Jennings, now used to life in Japan, looked forward to big years. Hasegawa, Noda, and Hoshino were joined by the club's most important addition, an American pitcher named Willie Fraser. Fraser was a tough New Yorker who could both start and relieve. And of course, big things were expected once again for the young man now known throughout Asia by his first name alone: Ichiro.

The Blue Wave was favored to win the Pacific League title, although probably not as easily as in

"That's incredible...but that's Ichiro for you."
PRIME MINISTER JUNICHIRO KOIZUMI

17

Ichiro legs out a hit during the 1996 season. He won the batting championship for the third year in a row.

1995. This proved to be the case, as they trailed Tokyo's Nippon Ham Fighters for most of the season. The Fighters were led by pitcher Kip Gross and sluggers Bernardo Brito, Yukio Tanaka, and Atsushi Kataoka. Not until late August did Orix pull even with the Fighters, but after that they opened up a seven-game lead and cruised to a second consecutive pennant. Neel won the league home run and RBI championships, while Ichiro took the batting crown with a .356 average. He also was tops with 193 hits and 104 runs, and won his third-straight MVP award.

In the Japan Series, the Blue Wave squared off against the Yomiuri Giants, the most famous team in the country. The Giants had looked dead in July, trailing the Central League-leading Hiroshima Carp by more than 10 games. But a furious comeback—led by MVP Hideki Matsui and the pitching duo of Balvino Galvez and Masaki Saito—brought the Giants their second pennant in three years.

The 1996 Japan Series was another five-game affair, only this time the Blue Wave won. Ichiro was cheered wildly whenever he came to the plate and whenever he tracked down a ball in the outfield. He reached base seven times in the series and hit a home run. Ichiro was happy that the team was able to clinch the championship at Green Stadium in Kobe. It was a nice gift for a city that was still suffering from the aftermath of the 1995 disaster.

Looking Past the Pacific

chapter 4

"I wanted the challenge of competing against the best players in the world."

— ICHIRO SUZIKI

ike every young Japanese star, there were times when Ichiro Suzuki squinted into the sunrise and wondered how much tougher baseball really was on the other side of the ocean. Bobby Valentine and other Americans with major-league experience had told him he was talented enough to make it in the big leagues. That meant a lot to Ichiro, but there were other things that made him wonder whether they were telling the truth. His teammate Troy Neel had dominated Pacific League pitching in 1996. In America, he had done the same in the minors, winning a Class-AA slugging championship and a Class-AAA batting

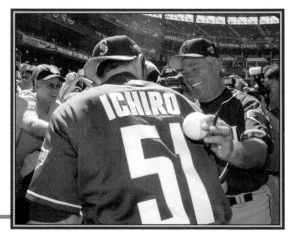

Ichiro and Bobby Valentine renew acquaintances at the 2001 All-Star Game. Valentine was one of the first Americans to tell him he could be a star in the majors.

Mike Piazza's praise of Ichiro caused quite a commotion.

championship. Yet in the majors, Neel had been just an ordinary hitter. Ichiro could not bear the thought of being considered "ordinary."

Following the 1996 season, an All-Star exhibition series against major-league players was held in Japan. Ichiro had a great series against the American stars. Mike Piazza, one of the best hitters ever to play the game, told the Japanese press that Ichiro was good enough to come to the majors right away. This caused great excitement. Even though Hideo Nomo had been successful in the majors, it was still believed that no Japanese position players were ready to make the jump.

When Ichiro was told of Piazza's remarks, he felt very proud and excited. An entire nation waited to hear how their hero would respond. As always, he had the perfect answer. "I could go," Ichiro smiled, "but I would be the bat boy."

Ichiro was joking, of course, but there was some truth to what he said. There really was no way of knowing how he

Did You Know?

In the early 1990s, when he first rose to stardom, Ichiro had signed a number of high-paying endorsement deals. By the late 1990s, he was a big enough name to market his own products. In 1997, he started his own clothing line. Within weeks, it was the top-selling brand in Japan.

*Ichiro shows off his opposite-field stroke during a 1997 game.
He knocked in a career-best 91 runs that season.*

would do in the major leagues. Anyway, it hardly mattered, for he would not be allowed to leave the Blue Waves until after the 2000 season, when he had played out his contract with the club.

In the meantime, Ichiro had another championship to win. The Blue Wave played well in 1997, but the Seibu Lions were rolling again and edged the Orix team for the Pacific League title by five games. Troy Neel had another nice season, but the other Americans failed to contribute as they had the year before.

Ichiro won his fourth-straight batting title with a .345 average, knocked in a career-best 91 runs, and set a league record by going 216 at bats without striking out. Yet despite leading the league in hits and runs again, he did not win the MVP. Instead, it went to pitcher Fumiya Nishiguchi of the Lions, the Central League's victory and strikeout leader. "Most Valuable" or not, Ichiro was still the talk of baseball. Against the

*Troy Neel (center) in his days with the A's. He helped power the
Orix lineup during its championship run.*

American All-Stars that fall, he batted .346 and stole bases at will. It was finally dawning on him that he might really be good enough to make it in the major leagues.

At the same time, Ichiro was starting to grow tired of the restrictions his fame was placing on his lifestyle. He was mobbed by adoring fans and autograph-seekers whenever he showed his face in public. Mail addressed simply "Ichiro/Japan" came from all over the world and arrived in bags at his home. His girlfriend, Yumiko Fukushima, a television sportscaster, was used to being recognized on the street and in restaurants. But trying to have a quiet date with Ichiro was now completely out of the question. When the two met someplace for dinner, they had to eat in a private room with guards outside. Once, Ichiro had to roll himself up in a carpet and have friends throw him in the back of a pickup truck so he could get to a meeting with Yumiko on time! After the 1997 season, Ichiro and Yumiko decided to get married. They feared that a wedding in

Japan might cripple the entire country, so they flew to Los Angeles, California (under fake names) and had the ceremony there.

The 1998 season found the Blue Wave struggling to win as often as it lost. Neel and Jennings had returned to the U.S. and were replaced with utility man Chris Donnels and outfielder Harvey Pulliam. Mark Mimbs and Edwin Hurtado joined Willie Fraser in the Orix pitching rotation, but the Japanese hurlers on the staff pitched poorly. The Seibu Lions ran away with the pennant, and the Blue Wave players just kind of lost interest. Even Ichiro was guilty of this. Although he won another batting title and led the league in hits again, he stole just 11 bases—a clear sign that he was bored. "I didn't lose my desire to play in Japan, but it wasn't interesting to me anymore," he admits.

The competition was no longer challenging. It was time to think more seriously about playing in North America. "I couldn't make my fans happy if I continued to play there," Ichiro explains. "I felt there was a need for something else."

The owners of the team knew this day would come. They set a plan in motion that would give Ichiro a chance to make it in the majors, while benefiting the Blue Wave, too. Through a process known as "posting," a club could hold a sealed-bid auction for the right to negotiate with one of its players as a free agent. There was no guarantee that a player would ink a contract with the new team, but whatever happened the Blue Wave could keep the money.

To start generating interest in America, the Blue Wave "loaned" three of its best players—Ichiro and pitchers Nobuyuki Hoshino and Nobuyuki Ebisu—to the Seattle Mariners during spring training of 1999. Ichiro fit right in during his short stay with the Mariners. Although he needed a translator in the clubhouse, he was able to

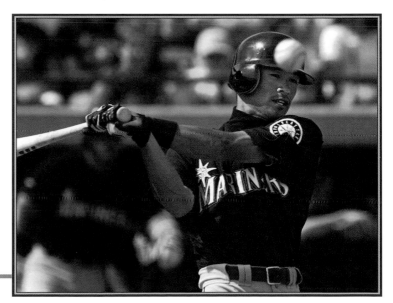

Ichiro takes a cut during his spring training stay with the Mariners.

> "When I took part in the Mariners camp in 1999, I felt like a rookie, almost like a little kid."
>
> **ICHIRO SUZUKI**

joke with his English- and Spanish-speaking teammates, and also exchange tips and advice. Ichiro was in heaven. He was playing again with passion and desire, and it showed. The Seattle players were very impressed.

"That guy can get after the ball," said Butch Huskey. "From what I've seen, he can track down just about anything."

"It was obvious from what we saw in camp that he's at an elite level," Jay Buhner remarked.

"He's a cool guy," added Ken Griffey Jr. "You can tell he has confidence in his ability."

"He had a flair to him," remembers manager Lou Piniella. "He carried himself like a superstar player. In fact, he reminded me of Carl Yastrzemski. He had the same gait, the same carriage."

As Ichiro packed his bags to return to Kobe, he knew where his future was. "I have enjoyed seeing players like Ken Griffey Jr. up close and comparing my game to theirs," he told the American writers. "If it's possible, I want to someday play in the United States."

Did You Know?

During his short stay with the Mariners in 1999, Ichiro noticed that the "looser" American players were, the better they performed. He had often wondered why Japanese baseball coaches acted as if every minute of a game was a life-and-death struggle. "Everybody in the states is so relaxed," he says, "and everybody in Japan is so uptight."

So Long, Farewell

"He told me that the major leagues is his type of baseball."

— ORIX TEAMMATE WILLIE BANKS

The 1999 season was not much fun. All Ichiro could think about was playing ball in the United States. Once again, the Blue Wave was basically a .500 team, and Ichiro missed the final five weeks with a broken wrist. Even so, he won the Pacific League batting title for the sixth time in a row.

Everyone in Japan knew the 2000 season would be Ichiro's last in a Blue Wave uniform. He was excited about playing ball in the United States in 2001, but sad about abandoning his loyal fans. He decided

"The skills he has translate into any league."
ALL-STAR BRADY ANDERSON

Ichiro appears with Seattle executive Howard Lincoln at a press conference. Most observers believed the Mariners had the inside track on the Japanese star's services.

to give them a season to remember, to try to break all of his records and lead the Blue Wave to the pennant again.

Unfortunately for the fans in Kobe, the Blue Wave just did not have the pitching to stay competitive. But Ichiro was simply phenomenal. He was making great catches, gunning out runners at every base, and batting over .400. His average might have stayed there were it not for a pulled muscle in his rib cage. The injury kept him out of many games during the second half of the season and made every swing a painful one.

"I want to be the first player to show what Japanese batters can do in the major leagues."
ICHIRO SUZUKI

Despite these obstacles, Ichiro still managed to break his own league record by hitting .387 for the year. It was his seventh-consecutive batting championship.

On November 1, 2000, the Blue Wave notified Hiromori Kawashima, the commissioner of Japanese baseball, that they planned to let Ichiro go to North America. Kawashima in turn contacted Bud Selig, the commissioner of Major League Baseball. He let interested clubs know they had 24 hours to make a secret bid for the privilege of negotiating with the Japanese star.

Ichiro had already hired an American agent named Tony Attanasio. Attanasio informed the different clubs that his client expected a generous contract, but made it clear that two other things would matter even more: Ichiro wanted to go to a winning team, and there had to be a strong Japanese community in that city. The Seattle Mariners, New York Mets, Los Angeles Dodgers, and Anaheim Angels decided they would submit bids.

On November 9, the bids were opened and the Seattle Mariners were declared the winner. They had decided to gamble more than $13 million that Ichiro would want to return to them for the 2001 season. Ichiro made it clear right away that he wanted to play in Seattle. There were several reasons the city made sense. A year earlier the team had signed Kazuhiro Sasaki, the greatest reliever in Japanese baseball (and a friend of Ichiro's). Sasaki quickly established

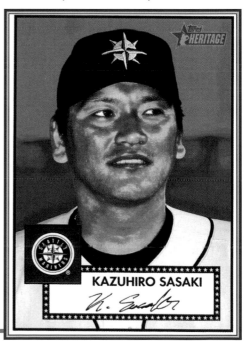

KAZUHIRO SASAKI

"Kazu" Sasaki made it into a Mariners uniform a year before his friend Ichiro.

japan league *stats*

Year	Team	G	AB	H	R	HR	RBI	SB	BA
1992	Orix Blue Wave	40	95	24	9	0	5	3	.253
1993	Orix Blue Wave	43	64	12	4	1	3	0	.188
1994	Orix Blue Wave	130	546*	210*	111*	13	54	29	.385*
1995	Orix Blue Wave	130	524	179*	104*	25	80*	49*	.342*
1996	Orix Blue Wave	130	542*	193*	104*	16	84	35	.356*
1997	Orix Blue Wave	135	536	185*	94*	17	91	39	.345*
1998	Orix Blue Wave	135	506	181*	79	13	71	11	.358*
1999	Orix Blue Wave	103	411	141	80	21	68	12	.343*
2000	Orix Blue Wave	105	395	153	73	12	74	21	.387*
Total		**951**	**3,619**	**1,278**	**658**	**118**	**529**	**199**	**.353***

• LED LEAGUE

japan league *achievements*

Pacific League Batting Champion 1994–2000
Pacific League Best Nine (All-Star) 1994–2000
Pacific League Gold Glove 1994–2000
Pacific League MVP 1994–1996

himself as a top closer, and was named American League Rookie of the Year. Also, the Mariners were partly owned by Nintendo, the Japanese video-game company. And finally, Seattle had a great Japanese community.

A posted player has only one month to reach agreement on a new contract, so Ichiro and the Mariners got right to work. They hammered out a three-year deal worth more than $20 million. The contract also included English lessons for Ichiro and his wife, a personal trainer, an interpreter, an annual housing allowance, four round-trip plane tickets from Japan to Seattle, and the use of a car during spring training and the regular season.

Ichiro did not say so, but there was one other thing he liked about going to the Mariners. During 2000, the team had traded Ken Griffey Jr. and allowed Alex Rodriguez to leave via free agency. A year-and-a-half earlier, Randy Johnson, baseball's most dominant pitcher, had been dealt away. That meant the pressure would really be on Ichiro to come through. And that is the kind of pressure he thrives on.

A Spring in His Step

chapter 6

"I've never seen anyone hit that way."
— TEAMMATE JOHN OLERUD

chiro got himself settled in Seattle before reporting to spring training with the Mariners. He and Yumiko stayed in a downtown hotel while they shopped for an apartment. They liked the city a lot. They especially enjoyed walking around town and eating meals in restaurants without being overwhelmed by fans. No one recognized Ichiro in Seattle. At least, not yet.

Ichiro left for the Mariners' camp in January, a few weeks before his teammates were scheduled to report. As he expected, there was already an enormous throng of reporters from Japan waiting for him. He had to laugh when they discovered that the

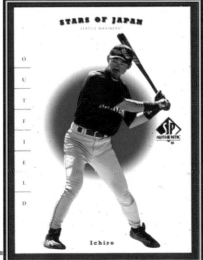

Months before his first official game, Ichiro's rookie card was one of the hottest in the hobby.

rules for the sports media are very different in America than they are in Japan. Reporters back home were much pushier, and were given free access to players. The Japanese news people were shocked and offended when the Mariners informed them they would have to follow a strict set of rules.

When the rest of the Mariners reported, Ichiro got to know the players and coaches, and began making the adjustments necessary to succeed in the majors. Mostly, he needed to get used to the way big-league pitchers throw. Compared to the ones he faced in Japan, they were bigger, threw harder, and had an extra pitch or two in their reper-

The Suzuki File

ICHIRO'S FAVORITE...

Sports to Watch	Track & Field
Video Game	Mario Bros.
Musician	Nelly
Cartoon	Dragon Ball Z
Food	Rice Balls
Baseball Player	Derek Jeter

*"I've always been very confident.
I'm just doing what
I know how to do."*

toires. There were also slight differences in the rhythm they had on the mound. All of these differences meant one thing: Ichiro would have to alter the timing of his swing.

Those who had seen tape of Ichiro's big leg kick thought this would be very hard to do. They pointed out that when you win seven batting titles hitting a certain way, you could lose your edge by making a big change. Ichiro had actually thought about this after his first trip to the United States, in 1999. During the 1999 and 2000 seasons, he had methodically reduced his leg kick and shortened his stride. By the time he signed, he was already used to this new style. It took him only a week or two of spring train-ing to make the final adjustments to his swing.

During that time, Ichiro hit the top of a lot of pitches, pounding them straight into the ground. To the untrained eye, it looked like something was wrong. But the coach-es trusted that he knew what he was doing and begged Ichiro's critics to be patient. Finally, with a few weeks to go, he began spraying line drives all over the place. And

*Ichiro zeroes in on a low pitch during spring training.
For several weeks he concentrated on staying "on top" of the ball.*

Ichiro's speed to first base amazed his teammates.

when he did get fooled, he hit high choppers that he beat out for infield singles. Everyone had heard so much about Ichiro's hitting and field-ing—they were blown away by his speed. From the time he hit the ball to the time he touched first base was a lightning-fast 3.7 to 3.8 seconds!

While American fans were beginning to gain an appreciation for Ichiro, Japanese fans were hanging on his every plate appearance—even though the spring train-ing games did not count. Seattle's first game of the exhibition season, a char-ity event against the San Diego Padres, was tele-vised live in Japan at 5:00 in the morning. Every baseball fan in the coun-try reported to work bleary-eyed that day.

TALE OF THE NUMBERS

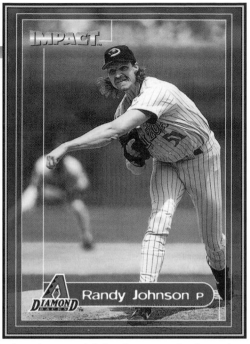

The Mariners assigned number 51 to Ichiro. That number had belonged to their greatest pitcher, Randy Johnson (right). Some said it should have been retired. Ichiro forwarded a personal message to the lanky left-hander. In it he promised that he "wouldn't bring shame to the number."

The man watching Ichiro with the most interest was his manager, Lou Piniella. He grew anxious during the early weeks of spring training, when his new player seemed content to tap high-hopping grounders to the infielders. Piniella was asked again and again how the seven-time batting champion would do in the Seattle lineup. He would not say, but stated that he would be happy if Ichiro hit .270 or .280. Piniella, like the rest of baseball, was in for a big surprise.

Manager Lou Piniella tried not to expect too much from Ichiro.

Flawless in Seattle

chapter 7

*"It's like every time
he gets on base,
he's going to score."*

— SUPERSTAR JASON GIAMBI

Anyone who was a baseball fan during the 2001 season probably knows what happened next. The Seattle Mariners, picked by many to finish third in the American League's Western Division, won more games than any team in league history. And their "Japanese import" hit a little better than the .270 or .280 his manager had hoped for—Ichiro led the American League with a .356 average! No one, not even the most optimistic fan of the Mariners or Ichiro, could have foreseen these developments. It was the kind of year that makes baseball such a magical sport.

With Ichiro igniting their offense from the leadoff spot, the Mariners started coming together as a team. What had once seemed like an average infield of John Olerud, Bret Boone, Carlos Guillen, and David Bell turned out to be an excellent one. Each player fielded his position well, and Boone hit like Babe Ruth. The team's outfield

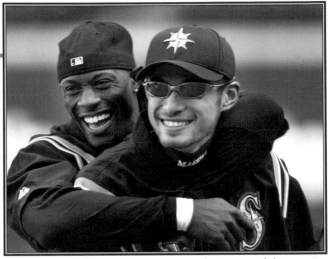

Mike Cameron and Ichiro became fast friends and team leaders.

also played above expectations. Center fielder Mike Cameron, a great glove man, blossomed into an All-Star hitter and a highly respected team leader. Left field was split between veterans Al Martin and Stan Javier, each of whom played solid defense and got clutch hits in key situations. In the heart of the batting order was Edgar Martinez, the greatest designated hitter in baseball history. With Ichiro and his teammates reaching base consistently, Martinez turned into an RBI machine.

The pitching staff was something special, too. Freddy Garcia, a tough-as-nails right-hander just coming into his prime, was the ace of a starting staff that included veterans Jamie Myer, Aaron Sele, and Paul Abbott. The bullpen featured four terrific set-up men, and the closer was Kazuhiro Sasaki. These hurlers were handled with great skill by catcher Dan Wilson.

Opening Day at Safeco Field found the Mariners playing the Oakland A's, a team that was supposed to finish far in front of Seattle in the standings. The game was carried live in Japan—on two different networks. Ichiro went hitless in his first three at bats, but then singled off T.J. Mathews to start a game-tying rally in the seventh inning. In the eighth inning, with the go-ahead run on base, Ichiro unveiled a

"The fact is, this guy could play when he got here, and he's going to be a great player in the major leagues for a long time. He knows his game. He knows his strengths. And he exploits them."
JASON GIAMBI

Ichiro drills a single on Opening Day against the Oakland A's.

weapon he had been secretly perfecting. He began leaning toward first base as the pitch arrived, then dropped his bat in front of the ball and sent it rolling between pitcher Jim Mecir and first baseman Jason Giambi. They were so shocked that they could not make a play, and Ichiro was safe. The winning run, now at third base, scored moments later on a sacrifice fly. Oakland manager Art Howe rifled through the scouting reports; they said that Ichiro had not bunted for a hit in eight years. Sasaki came in to slam the door with a save in the ninth inning, and the Mariners had their first of 116 victories.

Not surprisingly, Sasaki turned out to be Ichiro's most important teammate. Not only did he save 44 more games for the Mariners in 2001, he also told Ichiro what to expect from each new team they played and each new city they visited. He also advised his friend to learn to eat American food—because Japanese food would not always be available. "You'll like it," Sasaki promised.

When the Japanese media started hounding Ichiro outside the ballpark, Sasaki agreed to join him in a boycott against them. It was a brave thing to do, because fans back home did not look kindly upon defying the press. On Opening Day, however,

"Baseball has been the greatest thing in my life, but the cameras and the media surrounding baseball have not been fun. It's unnecessary. How many times do they see me stretch? How many times do they see me walk? It is a big concern. If it affected the team in a negative way, I don't know what I would do."

ICHIRO SUZUKI

both men had a good laugh as they trotted off the field. "A few years ago, Kazuhiro talked about how great it would be to play on the same team," says Ichiro, "to have a good game and have Kazu come in and save it. To have that happen in our first game was unbelievable."

In the next series, against the Rangers, Ichiro displayed another surprising side of his offensive arsenal when he blasted a game-winning two-run homer in the 11th inning. The Seattle writers who had nicknamed him the "Sultan of Slap" in training camp were forced to eat their words. When the situation called for a home run, Ichiro could turn on an inside fastball as well as anyone in the league.

The club traveled to New York a couple of weeks later with a 15–4 record. Just stepping onto the field in "The House That Ruth Built" was a big thrill for Ichiro. It was an even bigger thrill to leave Yankee Stadium with a three-game sweep. By the end of April, Seattle had won two more games, making it a record 20 victories for the month. Ichiro was named the American League's top rookie for April. His average was up around .400, and his confidence was sky-high. "It really helped that I got off to a good

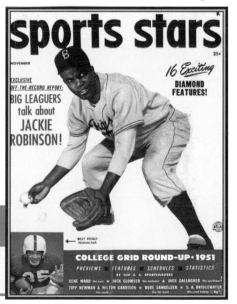

Did You Know?

Ichiro was the first player to lead the majors in hits and steals in the same year since Jackie Robinson in 1949.

Ichiro signs for the hometown fans prior to the 2001 All-Star Game. He received more votes than any other AL player.

start and that I was able to get so much support from the fans and my teammates," he says.

No one knew how to keep Ichiro off the bases. Enemy pitchers, watching how he moved toward first base as he swung, thought they could get him out with slow pitches on the outside part of the plate. Ichiro showed them why he was a seven-time batting champ: he instantly recognized the change of speed and drilled these pitches to left field. Yankee coach Don Zimmer, who has been analyzing baseball players for more than 50 years, watched Ichiro from the dugout during Seattle's sweep. Asked by reporters what he thought, Zimmer replied, "I would take him to win the batting title."

By the end of May, Ichiro and the Mariners had historians scrambling for the record books. The team was on pace to break the all-time record for victories, and Ichiro had a chance to break the all-time record for hits, held by Hall of Famer George Sisler. Meanwhile, Ichiro was receiving an avalanche of votes for the All-Star Game—which just happened to be scheduled for Seattle's Safeco Field.

Ichiro finished the season's first half with a .347 average and 28 stolen bases. He went into the All-Star Game as the league's top vote-getter. It marked the first time since 1964 that a rookie outfielder had made the AL's starting lineup. People the world over got to see Ichiro take his position in right field, with loyal fans behind him cheering his every move. They had renamed this section of Safeco Field "Area 51" in honor of his number. Ichiro beat out an infield single off Randy Johnson, and moments later scampered down to second base ahead of Mike Piazza's throw with the game's only stolen base.

Seattle continued to win at a record pace as the second half got under way. But at times it seemed that Ichiro was dragging. This was probably due to the demanding

pro stats

Year	Team	G	AB	H	R	HR	RBI	SB	BA
2001	Seattle Mariners	157	692*	242*	127	8	69	56*	.350*

• LED LEAGUE

pro achievements

American League All-Star 2001
American League Rookie of the Year 2001
American League Most Valuable Player 2001
Gold Glove Winner 2001

major-league schedule, which is 27 games longer than what he was used to. Lou Piniella, confident his team would win the division, began resting his key players. This worked wonders for Ichiro. After a much-needed day off, he went on a 21-game hitting streak. When it was done, Ichiro's average had climbed to .350. That is exactly where he finished the year to win the batting title. Including his Pacific League championships, that made eight in a row!

That was not all Ichiro won. He led the majors with 75 multihit games, 56 steals, and had the highest average in baseball with runners in scoring position (.445) and with the bases loaded (.545). He set an all-time record for hits by a rookie (242), and broke the league mark for singles in a season (192). He won a Gold Glove (he made just one error all year), took Rookie-of-the-Year honors, and edged Jason Giambi for the American League's Most Valuable Player award.

*Ichiro shares an **ESPN** cover with teammates Edgar Martinez, Mike Cameron, and Bret Boone. All would receive MVP votes at season's end.*

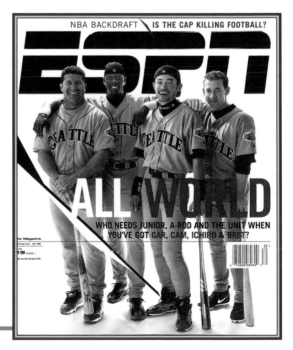

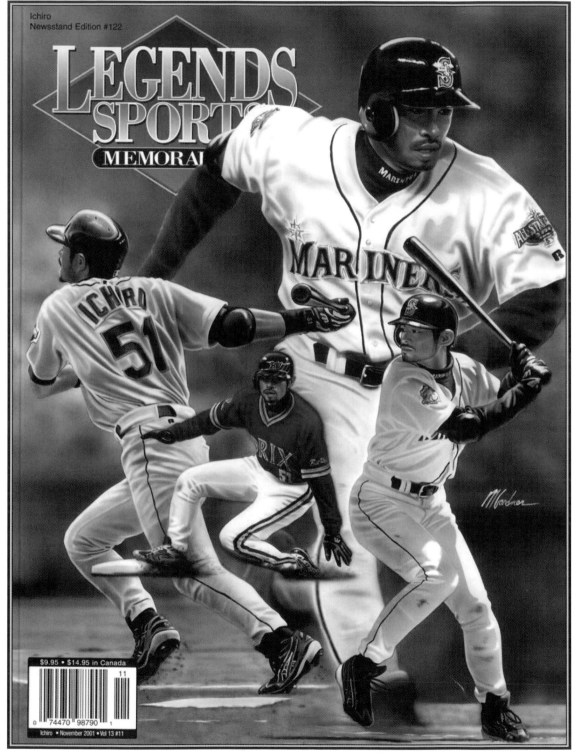

Ichiro
Newsstand Edition #122

LEGENDS SPORTS
MEMORA

$9.95 • $14.95 in Canada

0 74470 98790 1

Ichiro • November 2001 • Vol 13 #11

*Of all the magazine covers featuring Ichiro in 2001, the September
issue of LEGENDS SPORTS may have been the most striking.*

Team Player

chapter 8

"He's the
engine of our train."
— TEAMMATE MIKE CAMERON

In a Hollywood film, Ichiro Suzuki's 2001 season would have ended with a dramatic hit to win the World Series. This did not happen. Baseball's script is not written in a movie studio—it unfolds one pitch at a time on the baseball diamond.

Seattle needed to win the Division Series and the League Championship Series before getting into the Fall Classic, and they were nearly eliminated in the first round against the

Did You Know?

Ichiro batted safely in 135 games in 2001. That tied the all-time record, shared by Rogers Hornsby (right), Chuck Klein, Wade Boggs, and Derek Jeter.

Ichiro's offensive onslaught against the Indians helped Seattle reach the ALCS.

Cleveland Indians. The heavy-hitting Mariners struggled at the plate for the first time all season. They split the first two games of the best-of-five series, and then got bombed 17–2 in Game 3. Facing elimination, Seattle seemed helpless against Cleveland ace Bartolo Colon in Game 4. Finally, in the seventh inning, they loaded the bases with two out. Ichiro stepped to the plate with the season on the line. He calmly bounced a single into right field to give Seattle the lead and force a Game 5. In that contest, he scored the final run in a 3–1 victory. In all, Ichiro collected 12 hits in the series. His .600 average set a new record for Division Series play.

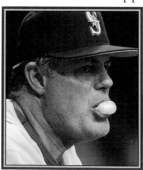

Did You Know?

Because he was on Japanese television so much, Seattle manager Lou Piniella (left) became a "cult figure" in Japan.

Bernie Williams blasts a homer against the Mariners in Game 4. His blow erased a lead that would have enabled the Mariners to tie the ALCS.

Against the Yankees—a team that had won three straight pennants—the Mariners finally met their match. The New Yorkers had great pitching and defense, and in a short series those weapons usually beat the kind of hitting Seattle had. The Yankees won the first two games, at Safeco Field, behind Andy Pettitte and Mike Mussina. Ichiro managed one meaningless hit in each contest. The Mariners bounced back to win Game 3 at Yankee Stadium, and were within five outs of evening the series in Game 4 when homers by Bernie Williams and Alfonso Soriano sent them to defeat. Game 5 was a 12–3 blowout in favor of the Yankees.

The Mariners were forced to fly home wondering what it meant to enjoy the record-smashing season they did, only to have it end this way. Ichiro knew what it meant. He had accomplished remarkable things as an individual—more than anyone could have imagined. Yet what made him truly proud about his first year as a major leaguer was what he achieved as a member of a team. In Japan, when the Blue Wave got into a tight spot, Ichiro knew everyone on the club looked for him to come up with the game-winning hit or the game-saving play. On this amazing Mariners team, no one person was expected to be the hero; each player looked within himself and tried to find some way to contribute.

Ichiro has the power to drive pitches over the fence. Scouts believe his homer totals will rise as he learns more about American League pitchers.

When Ichiro says he would "trade in all the awards for a World Series ring," he means it. What he *doesn't* say is that—given the chance to play for the team that *did* win the World Series—there is no way he would go back and trade his year with the Mariners for anything.

As the 2002 season opened, Ichiro was once again baseball's hottest topic. Some said he could break the all-time hit record, because he now knew AL pitchers so well. Others claimed that AL pitchers, with a whole year of videotape to study, would find a way to neutralize the Japanese star. Few who know Ichiro, however, believe he would ever allow an opposing hurler to gain the upper hand.

HIT PARADE

The ultimate "Rookie Card" collection has to begin with these six stars. They banged out more hits than any first-year players in history.

PLAYER	TEAM	YEAR	HITS
ICHIRO SUZUKI	MARINERS	2001	242
LLOYD WANER	PIRATES	1927	223
TONY OLIVA	TWINS	1964	217
DALE ALEXANDER	TIGERS	1929	215
JOHNNY FREDERICK	DODGERS	1929	209
HARVEY KUENN	TIGERS	1953	209

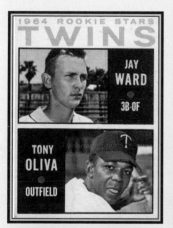

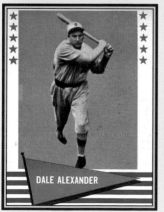

"Ichiro-mania"...Seattle style!

In Japan, the great debate centered on the effect that Ichiro's success might have on baseball in that country. Would all of the nation's best hitters now automatically jump to the majors? If so, wouldn't this ruin the quality of Japanese baseball?

Ichiro believes that the opposite is true. Although a handful of Japanese stars might choose to play in North America, many will stay in Japan, so the quality should remain high. Meanwhile, those who do play in the majors will eventually return to Japan and help the game evolve. "Those players can give something back to Japanese baseball," he says. "They can go back and play, or go back as coaches or managers."

For that reason alone, Ichiro maintains he will never regret his decision to come to America. He proved it could be done, opening up new horizons for others in his sport. In fact, if he never wins another batting championship or award—or fails to win a World Series—it does not matter. Getting to the majors meant everything to him; everything else was just icing on the cake.

"I had a dream," Ichiro says. "And I made that dream come true."

Relaxed and confident, Ichiro has become one of baseball's biggest stars—on both sides of the Pacific.

Index